NITTY-GRITTY RHYMING RIDDLE BOOK

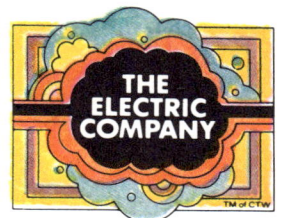
THE ELECTRIC COMPANY

by Sharon Lerner
Larry Ross drew the pictures

"A NITTY-GRITTY IS A RIDDLE WITH A TWO-WORD ANSWER THAT RHYMES."

Read each riddle and see if you can guess the rhyming answer before you turn the page! Then see if you can make up some Nitty-Gritties of your own.

AN ELECTRIC COMPANY BOOK • Published by Western Publishing Company, Inc., in conjunction with Children's Television Workshop. © 1973 Children's Television Workshop. All rights reserved. THE ELECTRIC COMPANY and THE ELECTRIC COMPANY SIGN are trademarks and service marks of Children's Television Workshop. GOLDEN and GOLDEN PRESS® are trademarks of Western Publishing Company, Inc. Printed in U.S.A.

A ship keeps warm in a boat coat.

And fish play baseball in a shark park.

So what did the king's wife turn into when she ate a rotten apple?

A gr**ee**n qu**ee**n!

What did the queen use to tie up her husband?

What do you use to weigh a very big sea animal?

What kind of bag do you use to carry a flock of noisy ducks?

A quack sack!

If Fargo North, Decoder, got sick for one hundred years, what would he have?

How do you clean a dirty rose?

Give it a flower shower!

Can you think of the nitty-gritty name for each picture?
Turn the page to check your answers.